# DO LATER!

## A 2013 Planner (or Non-Planner)
### for the
## Creative Procrastinator

*by* Mark Asher

*Pomegranate*

Catalog No. G030

Published by Pomegranate Communications, Inc.
Box 808022, Petaluma CA 94975

Available in the UK and mainland Europe from Pomegranate Europe Ltd.
Unit 1, Heathcote Business Centre, Hurlbutt Road, Warwick, Warwickshire CV34 6TD, UK

© 2012 Mark Asher

Pomegranate publishes a wide variety of wall, mini wall, and desk calendars. Our
extensive line of paper gift products and books can be found at retail stores throughout
the world and online. For more information or to place an order, please contact
Pomegranate Communications, Inc., 800 227 1428, www.pomegranate.com.

Designed by Patrice Morris

Dates in color indicate US federal holidays.
Dates listed for all astronomical events in this calendar are based on Coordinated Universal Time (UTC),
the worldwide system of civil timekeeping. UTC is essentially equivalent to Greenwich Mean Time.
Moon phases and American, Canadian, and UK holidays are noted.

 **NEW MOON**     **FIRST QUARTER**     **FULL MOON**     **LAST QUARTER**

# Welcome, Procrastinator!

To heck with hectic! Wouldn't you rather relax in a waiting room than be rushed into Emergency? Then you're among friends here. Step aside and slow down with a few relaxing breaths while the go-go-goers hurtle past in their panic. *Do It Later!* is designed for the way time-indifferent people work. (We're procrastinators—we get the important stuff done . . . when we get around to it.) To be productive and creative, we first need to engage in critical activities like cleaning our monitors and keyboards, organizing the items in our desk drawers, and checking and rechecking our e-mail. If you specialize in such delay tactics (or know someone who does), take a few minutes to flip through the tips and wisdom sprinkled throughout this planner ("The brain is a muscle that works best in short spurts"; "Start your most arduous tasks on Monday and finish them on Someday").

Then start by writing a to-do item in a section that makes sense, such as "Things I have to do but that can wait a day, or two, or three . . ."; or "Small things I have to do before I can do the big things I have to do"; or "Things I absolutely have to do unless I absolutely don't want to do them." *Do It Later!* is also filled with useful lists, like "How to Use Your Pet as a Procrastination Partner" and "Killer Excuses for Arriving Late at Work." There's even a place to keep track of due dates and grace periods for your bills, a space to plan those crucial tax extensions, room to list contact information for procrastination partners, and a weekly Doodle Block for that most beloved pastime of procrastinators.

Carry your new planner with pride. And if you never get around to starting the tasks you put in it—or even reading past this page—there's always tomorrow, or the day after, or . . .

—Mark Asher, fellow procrastinator

# Procrastinator Tip

Remember to stop, smell, prune, and photograph the roses along the way. You can count their petals, too.

**Things I have to do but that can wait a day, or two, or three . . .**

**Small things I have to do before I can do the big things I have to do**

**Things I absolutely have to do unless I absolutely don't want to do them**

**Things people have been bugging me to do for a really long time**

doodle block

# dec / jan

*monday*
**31** 366

NEW YEAR'S DAY
BANK HOLIDAY (CANADA, UK)
*tuesday*
**1** 1

BANK HOLIDAY (SCOTLAND)
*wednesday*
**2** 2

*thursday*
**3** 3

*friday*
**4** 4

*saturday*
◑ **5** 5

*sunday*
**6** 6

### january

| s | m | t | w | t | f | s |
|---|---|---|---|---|---|---|
|   |   |   | 1 | 2 | 3 | 4 | 5 |
| 6 | 7 | 8 | 9 | 10 | 11 | 12 |
| 13 | 14 | 15 | 16 | 17 | 18 | 19 |
| 20 | 21 | 22 | 23 | 24 | 25 | 26 |
| 27 | 28 | 29 | 30 | 31 |   |   |

# Procrastinator Tip

To be challenged or to be chill:
you decide.

**Things I have to do but that can wait a day, or two, or three . . .**

**Small things I have to do before I can do the big things I have to do**

**Things I absolutely have to do unless I absolutely don't want to do them**

**Things people have been bugging me to do for a really long time**

doodle block

# january

january

*monday*
## 7  7

*tuesday*
## 8  8

*wednesday*
## 9  9

*thursday*
## 10  10

*friday*
## ● 11  11

*saturday*
## 12  12

*sunday*
## 13  13

january

| s | m | t | w | t | f | s |
|---|---|---|---|---|---|---|
|   |   | 1 | 2 | 3 | 4 | 5 |
| 6 | 7 | 8 | 9 | 10 | 11 | 12 |
| 13 | 14 | 15 | 16 | 17 | 18 | 19 |
| 20 | 21 | 22 | 23 | 24 | 25 | 26 |
| 27 | 28 | 29 | 30 | 31 |   |   |

# Procrastinator Wisdom

Better not to do than to do and regret having done.

**Things I have to do but that can wait a day, or two, or three . . .**

**Small things I have to do before I can do the big things I have to do**

**Things I absolutely have to do unless I absolutely don't want to do them**

**Things people have been bugging me to do for a really long time**

# january

*monday*
14 14

*tuesday*
15 15

*wednesday*
16 16

*thursday*
17 17

*friday*
◐ 18 18

*saturday*
19 19

*sunday*
20 20

**january**

| s | m | t | w | t | f | s |
|---|---|---|---|---|---|---|
| | | 1 | 2 | 3 | 4 | 5 |
| 6 | 7 | 8 | 9 | 10 | 11 | 12 |
| 13 | 14 | 15 | 16 | 17 | 18 | 19 |
| 20 | 21 | 22 | 23 | 24 | 25 | 26 |
| 27 | 28 | 29 | 30 | 31 | | |

# Procrastinator Wisdom

Procrastination is a productive person's way of making sure there is always enough to do.

**Things I have to do but that can wait a day, or two, or three . . .**

**Small things I have to do before I can do the big things I have to do**

**Things I absolutely have to do unless I absolutely don't want to do them**

**Things people have been bugging me to do for a really long time**

doodle
block

# january

MARTIN LUTHER KING JR. DAY

*monday*
**21** 21

*tuesday*
**22** 22

*wednesday*
**23** 23

*thursday*
**24** 24

*friday*
**25** 25

*saturday*
**26** 26

*sunday*
○ **27** 27

## january

| s | m | t | w | t | f | s |
|---|---|---|---|---|---|---|
|   |   |   | 1 | 2 | 3 | 4 | 5 |
| 6 | 7 | 8 | 9 | 10 | 11 | 12 |
| 13 | 14 | 15 | 16 | 17 | 18 | 19 |
| 20 | 21 | 22 | 23 | 24 | 25 | 26 |
| 27 | 28 | 29 | 30 | 31 |   |   |

# Procrastinator Wisdom

A conscientious person waters the plants, pets the animals, comforts a neighbor, and calls at least one ailing relative or friend before beginning the day's work.

**Things I have to do but that can wait a day, or two, or three . . .**

**Small things I have to do before I can do the big things I have to do**

**Things I absolutely have to do unless I absolutely don't want to do them**

**Things people have been bugging me to do for a really long time**

doodle
block

# jan / feb

monday
## 28    28

tuesday
## 29    29

wednesday
## 30    30

thursday
## 31    31

friday
## 1    32

saturday
## 2    33

sunday
◑ **3**    34

february

| s | m | t | w | t | f | s |
|---|---|---|---|---|---|---|
|   |   |   |   |   | 1 | 2 |
| 3 | 4 | 5 | 6 | 7 | 8 | 9 |
| 10 | 11 | 12 | 13 | 14 | 15 | 16 |
| 17 | 18 | 19 | 20 | 21 | 22 | 23 |
| 24 | 25 | 26 | 27 | 28 |   |   |

# Procrastinator Wisdom

Obstacles are signposts telling you to slow down, have a rest, and rethink the path you are on.

Things I have to do but that can wait a day, or two, or three . . .

Small things I have to do before I can do the big things I have to do

Things I absolutely have to do unless I absolutely don't want to do them

Things people have been bugging me to do for a really long time

doodle block

# february

*monday*
4 35

*tuesday*
5 36

*wednesday*
6 37

*thursday*
7 38

*friday*
8 39

*saturday*
9 40

LUNAR NEW YEAR

*sunday*
● 10 41

### february

| s | m | t | w | t | f | s |
|---|---|---|---|---|---|---|
|   |   |   |   |   | 1 | 2 |
| 3 | 4 | 5 | 6 | 7 | 8 | 9 |
| 10 | 11 | 12 | 13 | 14 | 15 | 16 |
| 17 | 18 | 19 | 20 | 21 | 22 | 23 |
| 24 | 25 | 26 | 27 | 28 |   |   |

## Things to Do When There's No Emergency Beyond Avoiding the Things You Don't Want to Do

1. Do a dry run on packing up your valuables and evacuating your house. Feel free to take a celebratory joyride afterward.

2. Search online for exotic places to live in case you need to leave home temporarily.

3. Get on a first-name basis with all the employees of companies near yours. Offer them a tour of your office and discuss which items in your vending machines would be suitable for emergency rations.

4. Learn how to shut off your main water valve. While you're there, stop and think about new landscaping projects.

5. Scrub the filter beneath your water heater. Then take a hot bath to soak your back and knees.

6. Have all family members decorate their emergency face masks so they'll be easily identifiable in the event they are needed.

7. Sample different radio stations to find the best one for breaking news and vital information.

8. Download a flashlight app to your smartphone and practice finding your way around your house with all the lights turned off.

9. Devise fire escape plans for fires starting in 10 different places.

10. Go furniture shopping to scope out new pieces you'd buy if your place were damaged.

# List the first 10 things you would buy if you won the lottery tomorrow.

1. _____

2. _____

3. _____

4. _____

5. _____

6. _____

7. _____

8. _____

9. _____

10. _____

# Procrastinator Tip

Back in the good old days, a procrastinator was referred to as an easygoing, well-adjusted person.

Things I have to do but that can wait a day, or two, or three . . .

Small things I have to do before I can do the big things I have to do

Things I absolutely have to do unless I absolutely don't want to do them

Things people have been bugging me to do for a really long time

doodle block

# february

monday
**11** 42

MARDI GRAS
tuesday
**12** 43

ASH WEDNESDAY
wednesday
**13** 44

VALENTINE'S DAY
thursday
**14** 45

friday
**15** 46

saturday
**16** 47

sunday
◑ **17** 48

## february

| s | m | t | w | t | f | s |
|---|---|---|---|---|---|---|
|   |   |   |   |   | 1 | 2 |
| 3 | 4 | 5 | 6 | 7 | 8 | 9 |
| 10 | 11 | 12 | 13 | 14 | 15 | 16 |
| 17 | 18 | 19 | 20 | 21 | 22 | 23 |
| 24 | 25 | 26 | 27 | 28 |   |   |

# Procrastinator Tip

Uncompleted tasks are biodegradable and disintegrate over time.

Things I have to do but that can wait a day, or two, or three . . .

Small things I have to do before I can do the big things I have to do

Things I absolutely have to do unless I absolutely don't want to do them

Things people have been bugging me to do for a really long time

doodle block

# february

| | | |
|---|---|---|
| PRESIDENTS' DAY | *monday* | |
| FAMILY DAY (CANADA, SOME PROVINCES) | **18** | 49 |

| | | |
|---|---|---|
| | *tuesday* | |
| | **19** | 50 |

| | | |
|---|---|---|
| | *wednesday* | |
| | **20** | 51 |

| | | |
|---|---|---|
| | *thursday* | |
| | **21** | 52 |

| | | |
|---|---|---|
| | *friday* | |
| | **22** | 53 |

| | | |
|---|---|---|
| PURIM (BEGINS AT SUNSET) | *saturday* | |
| | **23** | 54 |

| | | |
|---|---|---|
| | *sunday* | |
| | **24** | 55 |

**february**

| s | m | t | w | t | f | s |
|---|---|---|---|---|---|---|
| | | | | | 1 | 2 |
| 3 | 4 | 5 | 6 | 7 | 8 | 9 |
| 10 | 11 | 12 | 13 | 14 | 15 | 16 |
| 17 | 18 | 19 | 20 | 21 | 22 | 23 |
| 24 | 25 | 26 | 27 | 28 | | |

# Procrastinator Wisdom

 Procrastination is the reward for a life of endless anticipation.

**Things I have to do but that can wait a day, or two, or three . . .**

**Small things I have to do before I can do the big things I have to do**

**Things I absolutely have to do unless I absolutely don't want to do them**

**Things people have been bugging me to do for a really long time**

doodle block

monday
○ 25  56

tuesday
26  57

wednesday
27  58

thursday
28  59

friday
1  60

saturday
2  61

sunday
3  62

march

| s | m | t | w | t | f | s |
|---|---|---|---|---|---|---|
|   |   |   |   |   | 1 | 2 |
| 3 | 4 | 5 | 6 | 7 | 8 | 9 |
| 10 | 11 | 12 | 13 | 14 | 15 | 16 |
| 17 | 18 | 19 | 20 | 21 | 22 | 23 |
| 24 | 25 | 26 | 27 | 28 | 29 | 30 |
| 31 |   |   |   |   |   |   |

# Procrastinator Tip

Whatever your reason for not doing something—laziness, fear of failure, perfectionism—honor it and love thyself.

**Things I have to do but that can wait a day, or two, or three . . .**

**Small things I have to do before I can do the big things I have to do**

**Things I absolutely have to do unless I absolutely don't want to do them**

**Things people have been bugging me to do for a really long time**

doodle block

M

# march

*tuesday*

**5** 64

*wednesday*

**6** 65

*thursday*

**7** 66

INTERNATIONAL WOMEN'S DAY

*friday*

**8** 67

*saturday*

**9** 68

DAYLIGHT SAVING TIME BEGINS
MOTHERING SUNDAY (UK)

*sunday*

**10** 69

### march

| s | m | t | w | t | f | s |
|---|---|---|---|---|---|---|
|   |   |   |   |   | 1 | 2 |
| 3 | 4 | 5 | 6 | 7 | 8 | 9 |
| 10 | 11 | 12 | 13 | 14 | 15 | 16 |
| 17 | 18 | 19 | 20 | 21 | 22 | 23 |
| 24 | 25 | 26 | 27 | 28 | 29 | 30 |
| 31 |   |   |   |   |   |   |

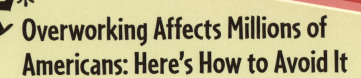

# Overworking Affects Millions of Americans: Here's How to Avoid It

1. Have a chatty friend call to check on you every couple of hours.

2. Set your alarm to go off every three hours to a loud rock station and play some air guitar.

3. If you work at home, put a sign on your front door that says "Solicitors Welcome." If you work in an office, put up a sign that says "Visitors Welcome."

4. Always leave your workplace for lunch and take a long walk afterward to digest your food.

5. Sign up for several daily e-mail newsletters to balance your work with interesting reading.

6. Make your work chair as comfortable as possible to invite sleep if the body needs it.

7. Do occasional market research at your local mall or favorite store.

8. Sit at your desk with a pad of paper and a pen or pencil and gaze thoughtfully at the paper, tapping your pen or pencil. This is called brainstorming.

9. Form a daily meditation group at work, but allow people to lie down while they meditate.

10. Reward the completion of every work project with an office party.

# Make a list of travel apps to download that will entice you to take a vacation.

1. _____

2. _____

3. _____

4. _____

5. _____

6. _____

7. _____

8. _____

9. _____

10. _____

# Procrastinator Wisdom

Doing nothing is doing something, but doing something can sometimes feel like doing nothing.

Things I have to do but that can wait a day, or two, or three . . .

Small things I have to do before I can do the big things I have to do

Things I absolutely have to do unless I absolutely don't want to do them

Things people have been bugging me to do for a really long time

doodle
block

# march

tuesday
12  71

wednesday
13  72

thursday
14  73

friday
15  74

saturday
16  75

march

| s | m | t | w | t | f | s |
|---|---|---|---|---|---|---|
|   |   |   |   |   | 1 | 2 |
| 3 | 4 | 5 | 6 | 7 | 8 | 9 |
| 10 | 11 | 12 | 13 | 14 | 15 | 16 |
| 17 | 18 | 19 | 20 | 21 | 22 | 23 |
| 24 | 25 | 26 | 27 | 28 | 29 | 30 |
| 31 |   |   |   |   |   |   |

ST. PATRICK'S DAY

sunday
17  76

# Procrastinator Wisdom

If cleanliness is next to godliness, then spending an entire day cleaning should be viewed as a religious experience and not an act of procrastination.

**Things I have to do but that can wait a day, or two, or three . . .**

**Small things I have to do before I can do the big things I have to do**

**Things I absolutely have to do unless I absolutely don't want to do them**

**Things people have been bugging me to do for a really long time**

doodle block

# march

*tuesday*
◐ **19** 78

VERNAL EQUINOX 11:02 UTC

*wednesday*
**20** 79

*thursday*
**21** 80

*friday*
**22** 81

*saturday*
**23** 82

**march**

| s | m | t | w | t | f | s |
|---|---|---|---|---|---|---|
|   |   |   |   |   | 1 | 2 |
| 3 | 4 | 5 | 6 | 7 | 8 | 9 |
| 10 | 11 | 12 | 13 | 14 | 15 | 16 |
| 17 | 18 | 19 | 20 | 21 | 22 | 23 |
| 24 | 25 | 26 | 27 | 28 | 29 | 30 |
| 31 |   |   |   |   |   |   |

PALM SUNDAY

*sunday*
**24** 83

# Procrastinator Wisdom

Hard work pays off in time; procrastination is instant gratification.

Things I have to do but that can wait a day, or two, or three . . .

Small things I have to do before I can do the big things I have to do

Things I absolutely have to do unless I absolutely don't want to do them

Things people have been bugging me to do for a really long time

doodle block

PASSOVER (BEGINS AT SUNSET)

*monday*
## 25 84

*tuesday*
## 26 85

*wednesday*
## ○ 27 86

*thursday*
## 28 87

GOOD FRIDAY
BANK HOLIDAY (CANADA, UK)

*friday*
## 29 88

*saturday*
## 30 89

### march

| s | m | t | w | t | f | s |
|---|---|---|---|---|---|---|
|   |   |   |   |   | 1 | 2 |
| 3 | 4 | 5 | 6 | 7 | 8 | 9 |
| 10 | 11 | 12 | 13 | 14 | 15 | 16 |
| 17 | 18 | 19 | 20 | 21 | 22 | 23 |
| 24 | 25 | 26 | 27 | 28 | 29 | 30 |
| 31 |   |   |   |   |   |   |

EASTER
SUMMER TIME BEGINS (UK)

*sunday*
## 31 90

# Procrastinator Tip

Better to do nothing, and avoid looking bad, than to proceed and look like a total idiot.

**Things I have to do but that can wait a day, or two, or three . . .**

**Small things I have to do before I can do the big things I have to do**

**Things I absolutely have to do unless I absolutely don't want to do them**

**Things people have been bugging me to do for a really long time**

doodle block

# april

EASTER MONDAY (CANADA, UK EXCEPT SCOTLAND)

*monday*
1  91

*tuesday*
2  92

*wednesday*
◑ 3  93

*thursday*
4  94

*friday*
5  95

*saturday*
6  96

*sunday*
7  97

## april

| s | m | t | w | t | f | s |
|---|---|---|---|---|---|---|
|   | 1 | 2 | 3 | 4 | 5 | 6 |
| 7 | 8 | 9 | 10 | 11 | 12 | 13 |
| 14 | 15 | 16 | 17 | 18 | 19 | 20 |
| 21 | 22 | 23 | 24 | 25 | 26 | 27 |
| 28 | 29 | 30 | | | | |

# How to Use Your Pet as a Procrastination Partner

1. Watch an online instructional video on the proper technique for cutting your dog or cat's nails and cleaning his ears.

2. Walk your dog forward and backward.

3. Create 26 nicknames for your pet, one starting with each letter of the alphabet.

4. Teach your cat how to fetch. Good luck.

5. Take your dog bed shopping and let her try out several different options in several different stores. Then write a blog on your findings.

6. Take your pet to be groomed. While waiting, shop for new pet toys, even though the ones you already have are of no interest to your pet.

7. Teach your cat how to shake hands. Good luck.

8. Brush your pet and collect the fur. Stuff pillows with it for holiday gifts.

9. Organize a "Bring Your Pet to Work Day." Allow stuffed animals.

10. Sit with your pet in a comfortable place and read *Moby Dick* out loud.

# List 10 killer dishes you'd request if you had your own personal chef.

1. _____

2. _____

3. _____

4. _____

5. _____

6. _____

7. _____

8. _____

9. _____

10. _____

# Procrastinator Tip

Where to start? That's always the question. "With something yummy to eat" is usually the answer.

**Things I have to do but that can wait a day, or two, or three . . .**

**Small things I have to do before I can do the big things I have to do**

**Things I absolutely have to do unless I absolutely don't want to do them**

**Things people have been bugging me to do for a really long time**

doodle block

# april

monday
**8** 98

tuesday
**9** 99

wednesday
● **10** 100

thursday
**11** 101

friday
**12** 102

saturday
**13** 103

sunday
**14** 104

## april

| s | m | t | w | t | f | s |
|---|---|---|---|---|---|---|
|   | 1 | 2 | 3 | 4 | 5 | 6 |
| 7 | 8 | 9 | 10 | 11 | 12 | 13 |
| 14 | 15 | 16 | 17 | 18 | 19 | 20 |
| 21 | 22 | 23 | 24 | 25 | 26 | 27 |
| 28 | 29 | 30 |   |   |   |   |

# Procrastinator Wisdom

When procrastination meets motivation, they usually meet at the mall.

Things I have to do but that can wait a day, or two, or three . . .

Small things I have to do before I can do the big things I have to do

Things I absolutely have to do unless I absolutely don't want to do them

Things people have been bugging me to do for a really long time

doodle block

*monday*
**15**  105

*tuesday*
**16**  106

*wednesday*
**17**  107

*thursday*
◑ **18**  108

*friday*
**19**  109

*saturday*
**20**  110

*sunday*
**21**  111

## april

| s | m | t | w | t | f | s |
|---|---|---|---|---|---|---|
|   |   | 1 | 2 | 3 | 4 | 5 | 6 |
| 7 | 8 | 9 | 10 | 11 | 12 | 13 |
| 14 | 15 | 16 | 17 | 18 | 19 | 20 |
| 21 | 22 | 23 | 24 | 25 | 26 | 27 |
| 28 | 29 | 30 |   |   |   |   |

# Procrastinator Wisdom

They say if you tackle your most difficult task first, nothing else will seem as hard. Considering I go to sleep after most difficult tasks, I guess they're right!

**Things I have to do but that can wait a day, or two, or three . . .**

**Small things I have to do before I can do the big things I have to do**

**Things I absolutely have to do unless I absolutely don't want to do them**

**Things people have been bugging me to do for a really long time**

doodle block

# april

EARTH DAY

**monday**
**22** 112

**tuesday**
**23** 113

**wednesday**
**24** 114

**thursday**
○ **25** 115

**friday**
**26** 116

**saturday**
**27** 117

**sunday**
**28** 118

**april**

| s | m | t | w | t | f | s |
|---|---|---|---|---|---|---|
|   |   | 1 | 2 | 3 | 4 | 5 | 6 |
| 7 | 8 | 9 | 10 | 11 | 12 | 13 |
| 14 | 15 | 16 | 17 | 18 | 19 | 20 |
| 21 | 22 | 23 | 24 | 25 | 26 | 27 |
| 28 | 29 | 30 |   |   |   |   |

# Procrastinator Tip

Imagine a world with no watches or clocks. It's easy if you try.

**Things I have to do but that can wait a day, or two, or three . . .**

**Small things I have to do before I can do the big things I have to do**

**Things I absolutely have to do unless I absolutely don't want to do them**

**Things people have been bugging me to do for a really long time**

doodle
block

*monday*
**29**  119

*tuesday*
**30**  120

*wednesday*
**1**  121

*thursday*
◑ **2**  122

*friday*
**3**  123

*saturday*
**4**  124

**may**

| s | m | t | w | t | f | s |
|---|---|---|---|---|---|---|
|   |   |   | 1 | 2 | 3 | 4 |
| 5 | 6 | 7 | 8 | 9 | 10 | 11 |
| 12 | 13 | 14 | 15 | 16 | 17 | 18 |
| 19 | 20 | 21 | 22 | 23 | 24 | 25 |
| 26 | 27 | 28 | 29 | 30 | 31 |   |

CINCO DE MAYO

*sunday*
**5**  125

# Procrastinator Wisdom

A fool shovels snow; a wise man waits for it to melt.

**Things I have to do but that can wait a day, or two, or three . . .**

**Small things I have to do before I can do the big things I have to do**

**Things I absolutely have to do unless I absolutely don't want to do them**

**Things people have been bugging me to do for a really long time**

doodle block

# may

BANK HOLIDAY (UK)              *monday*
## 6   126

*tuesday*
## 7   127

*wednesday*
## 8   128

*thursday*
## 9   129

*friday*
● 10   130

*saturday*
## 11   131

MOTHER'S DAY              *sunday*
## 12   132

**may**

| s | m | t | w | t | f | s |
|---|---|---|---|---|---|---|
|   |   |   | 1 | 2 | 3 | 4 |
| 5 | 6 | 7 | 8 | 9 | 10 | 11 |
| 12 | 13 | 14 | 15 | 16 | 17 | 18 |
| 19 | 20 | 21 | 22 | 23 | 24 | 25 |
| 26 | 27 | 28 | 29 | 30 | 31 |   |

# 10 Reasonable Reasons to Continue Procrastinating

1. You fear that if you finish your work early, it will be stale by the time it is due.

2. You'll lose the adrenaline rush of completing tasks at the last minute and might search for a less healthy addiction.

3. Becoming more efficient would only ruin your reputation as a slacker, and coworkers wouldn't stop by to swap jokes anymore.

4. You've tried ending your errant ways, and now you know that's no way to live.

5. If you turn your work in on time, your only reward will be more work.

6. The pain of doing something you don't want to do far exceeds the guilt of not doing it.

7. All the overly competent people in your life will say, "It's about time you came around." Why give them any satisfaction?

8. When you do things in a timely and organized manner, you feel out of place, odd, and slightly nauseated. It's important to be true to your own beautiful self.

9. Your mother loves you just the way you are.

10. Your pet loves you just the way you are, especially when you lie down for a nap rather than sit at your desk.

# Make a list of the scariest movies you've ever seen.

1. _____

2. _____

3. _____

4. _____

5. _____

6. _____

7. _____

8. _____

9. _____

10. _____

# Procrastinator Wisdom

People who dillydally are so plentiful, they have their own country—
ProcrastiNation.

**Things I have to do but that can wait a day, or two, or three . . .**

**Small things I have to do before I can do the big things I have to do**

**Things I absolutely have to do unless I absolutely don't want to do them**

**Things people have been bugging me to do for a really long time**

doodle
block

# may

*monday*
**13**  133

*tuesday*
**14**  134

*wednesday*
**15**  135

*thursday*
**16**  136

*friday*
**17**  137

ARMED FORCES DAY

*saturday*
◑ **18**  138

*sunday*
**19**  139

## may

| s | m | t | w | t | f | s |
|---|---|---|---|---|---|---|
|   |   |   | 1 | 2 | 3 | 4 |
| 5 | 6 | 7 | 8 | 9 | 10 | 11 |
| 12 | 13 | 14 | 15 | 16 | 17 | 18 |
| 19 | 20 | 21 | 22 | 23 | 24 | 25 |
| 26 | 27 | 28 | 29 | 30 | 31 |   |

# Procrastinator Wisdom

I'd rather be a free spirit than a working stiff.

**Things I have to do but that can wait a day, or two, or three . . .**

**Small things I have to do before I can do the big things I have to do**

**Things I absolutely have to do unless I absolutely don't want to do them**

**Things people have been bugging me to do for a really long time**

doodle block

VICTORIA DAY (CANADA)

*monday*
**20** 140

*tuesday*
**21** 141

*wednesday*
**22** 142

*thursday*
**23** 143

*friday*
**24** 144

*saturday*
○ **25** 145

*sunday*
**26** 146

## may

| s | m | t | w | t | f | s |
|---|---|---|---|---|---|---|
|   |   |   |   | 1 | 2 | 3 | 4 |
| 5 | 6 | 7 | 8 | 9 | 10 | 11 |
| 12 | 13 | 14 | 15 | 16 | 17 | 18 |
| 19 | 20 | 21 | 22 | 23 | 24 | 25 |
| 26 | 27 | 28 | 29 | 30 | 31 |   |

# Procrastinator Wisdom

An overproductive person thinks: "The longer I wait, the worse it gets." A procrastinator thinks: "The longer I wait, the more likely I'll forget about it or someone else will do it."

**Things I have to do but that can wait a day, or two, or three . . .**

**Small things I have to do before I can do the big things I have to do**

**Things I absolutely have to do unless I absolutely don't want to do them**

**Things people have been bugging me to do for a really long time**

doodle block

# may / jun

MEMORIAL DAY
BANK HOLIDAY (UK)

*monday*
**27** 147

*tuesday*
**28** 148

*wednesday*
**29** 149

*thursday*
**30** 150

*friday*
◑ **31** 151

*saturday*
**1** 152

*sunday*
**2** 153

# Procrastinator Wisdom

 I'm not feeling overwhelmed, and I'm not afraid of failure; I simply don't want to do anything!

**Things I have to do but that can wait a day, or two, or three . . .**

**Small things I have to do before I can do the big things I have to do**

**Things I absolutely have to do unless I absolutely don't want to do them**

**Things people have been bugging me to do for a really long time**

doodle block

# june

*monday*

3   154

*tuesday*

4   155

*wednesday*

5   156

*thursday*

6   157

*friday*

7   158

*saturday*

● 8   159

*sunday*

9   160

## june

| s | m | t | w | t | f | s |
|---|---|---|---|---|---|---|
|   |   |   |   |   |   | 1 |
| 2 | 3 | 4 | 5 | 6 | 7 | 8 |
| 9 | 10 | 11 | 12 | 13 | 14 | 15 |
| 16 | 17 | 18 | 19 | 20 | 21 | 22 |
| 23 | 24 | 25 | 26 | 27 | 28 | 29 |
| 30 |   |   |   |   |   |   |

# The Best Ways to Clear a Cluttered Mind

1. Lie on your side and imagine all your worries, woes, and work deadlines draining out of your ear. Then roll over and do it on the other side. This will empty both left and right brains.

2. Make a paper airplane out of your to-do list and fly it off a tall bridge.

3. Leave your office and walk around a one-mile radius, stopping every 50 steps and sitting down for 10 minutes. If you happen to stop in front of a coffee shop or bar, so be it.

4. Close your door, turn on some New Age music, and do a headstand. If you can't manage that, try to touch your toes instead. Don't pull a hammy.

5. Throw darts (or anything else you would like) at an image of a clock.

6. Learn how to say "Work does not define me; therefore I am free" in 10 different languages.

7. Every time you think about work, sing the first song that pops into your head, unless it's "The Little Drummer Boy." (Oops, now that's in your head. Sorry.)

8. Let your mind go on a fantasy vacation and imagine what you'll order for room service.

9. Eat some cookies. Really. This works.

10. Watch a cloud until it dissipates or drifts away. Then write a haiku about it.

**List 10 names you find distinguished and worthy of taking as your own. Don't forget to use peculiar middle names like Hiltrudis or Vanveren.**

1. _____

2. _____

3. _____

4. _____

5. _____

6. _____

7. _____

8. _____

9. _____

10. _____

# Procrastinator Wisdom

It isn't considered daydreaming if you do it at night.

**Things I have to do but that can wait a day, or two, or three . . .**

**Small things I have to do before I can do the big things I have to do**

**Things I absolutely have to do unless I absolutely don't want to do them**

**Things people have been bugging me to do for a really long time**

doodle block

# june

*monday*
**10**  161

*tuesday*
**11**  162

*wednesday*
**12**  163

*thursday*
**13**  164

FLAG DAY                                    *friday*
**14**  165

*saturday*
**15**  166

FATHER'S DAY                                *sunday*
◐ **16**  167

## june

| s | m | t | w | t | f | s |
|---|---|---|---|---|---|---|
|   |   |   |   |   |   | 1 |
| 2 | 3 | 4 | 5 | 6 | 7 | 8 |
| 9 | 10 | 11 | 12 | 13 | 14 | 15 |
| 16 | 17 | 18 | 19 | 20 | 21 | 22 |
| 23 | 24 | 25 | 26 | 27 | 28 | 29 |
| 30 |   |   |   |   |   |   |

# Procrastinator Tip

Studies show that an afternoon nap can increase productivity. Imagine what sleeping all day could do!

**Things I have to do but that can wait a day, or two, or three . . .**

**Small things I have to do before I can do the big things I have to do**

**Things I absolutely have to do unless I absolutely don't want to do them**

**Things people have been bugging me to do for a really long time**

doodle block

# june

---

*monday*
## 17 <small>168</small>

---

*tuesday*
## 18 <small>169</small>

---

*wednesday*
## 19 <small>170</small>

---

*thursday*
## 20 <small>171</small>

---

SUMMER SOLSTICE 05:04 UTC

*friday*
## 21 <small>172</small>

---

*saturday*
## 22 <small>173</small>

---

*sunday*
## ○ 23 <small>174</small>

**june**

| s | m | t | w | t | f | s |
|---|---|---|---|---|---|---|
|   |   |   |   |   |   | 1 |
| 2 | 3 | 4 | 5 | 6 | 7 | 8 |
| 9 | 10 | 11 | 12 | 13 | 14 | 15 |
| 16 | 17 | 18 | 19 | 20 | 21 | 22 |
| 23 | 24 | 25 | 26 | 27 | 28 | 29 |
| 30 |   |   |   |   |   |   |

# Procrastinator Tip

Start your most arduous tasks on Monday and finish them on Someday.

**Things I have to do but that can wait a day, or two, or three . . .**

**Small things I have to do before I can do the big things I have to do**

**Things I absolutely have to do unless I absolutely don't want to do them**

**Things people have been bugging me to do for a really long time**

doodle block

# june

monday
**24** 175

tuesday
**25** 176

wednesday
**26** 177

thursday
**27** 178

friday
**28** 179

saturday
**29** 180

sunday
◑ **30** 181

## june

| s | m | t | w | t | f | s |
|---|---|---|---|---|---|---|
|   |   |   |   |   |   | 1 |
| 2 | 3 | 4 | 5 | 6 | 7 | 8 |
| 9 | 10 | 11 | 12 | 13 | 14 | 15 |
| 16 | 17 | 18 | 19 | 20 | 21 | 22 |
| 23 | 24 | 25 | 26 | 27 | 28 | 29 |
| 30 |   |   |   |   |   |   |

# Procrastinator Wisdom

When a wise man told me to live each day as if it were my last, that was the last day I worked.

**Things I have to do but that can wait a day, or two, or three . . .**

**Small things I have to do before I can do the big things I have to do**

**Things I absolutely have to do unless I absolutely don't want to do them**

**Things people have been bugging me to do for a really long time**

doodle block

# july

CANADA DAY (CANADA)

*monday*
**1** 182

*tuesday*
**2** 183

*wednesday*
**3** 184

INDEPENDENCE DAY

*thursday*
**4** 185

*friday*
**5** 186

*saturday*
**6** 187

*sunday*
**7** 188

## july

| s | m | t | w | t | f | s |
|---|---|---|---|---|---|---|
|   | 1 | 2 | 3 | 4 | 5 | 6 |
| 7 | 8 | 9 | 10 | 11 | 12 | 13 |
| 14 | 15 | 16 | 17 | 18 | 19 | 20 |
| 21 | 22 | 23 | 24 | 25 | 26 | 27 |
| 28 | 29 | 30 | 31 |   |   |   |

## What to Say When Your Work Is Due and You're Not Done

1. I waited for the moment to act, but it was delayed by weather, as evidenced here on my smartphone's weather alert app.

2. I had every intention of finishing my project, but the thief of time robbed me again.

3. I worked like a dog before realizing that dogs don't work that hard.

4. All good things come to those who wait.

5. Endings make me emotional—I'm having a hard time finishing up.

6. I'd tell you why my work isn't done, but then I'd have to kill you.

7. Would it help if I told you the part I've finished is really good?

8. Would it ease your anger if you saw how clean my office is?

9. I fought myself to finish my work, and I lost.

10. I sprained my willpower muscle.

# List the first 10 laws you'd introduce if you were president of the United States.

1. _____

2. _____

3. _____

4. _____

5. _____

6. _____

7. _____

8. _____

9. _____

10. _____

# Procrastinator Wisdom

 It's better to start 15 things and not finish 1 than to finish 1 thing and miss out on starting 14.

**Things I have to do but that can wait a day, or two, or three . . .**

**Small things I have to do before I can do the big things I have to do**

**Things I absolutely have to do unless I absolutely don't want to do them**

**Things people have been bugging me to do for a really long time**

doodle block

# july

*monday*
● **8** 189

*tuesday*
**9** 190

*wednesday*
**10** 191

*thursday*
**11** 192

BANK HOLIDAY (N. IRELAND)
*friday*
**12** 193

*saturday*
**13** 194

*sunday*
**14** 195

## july

| s | m | t | w | t | f | s |
|---|---|---|---|---|---|---|
|   |   | 1 | 2 | 3 | 4 | 5 | 6 |
| 7 | 8 | 9 | 10 | 11 | 12 | 13 |
| 14 | 15 | 16 | 17 | 18 | 19 | 20 |
| 21 | 22 | 23 | 24 | 25 | 26 | 27 |
| 28 | 29 | 30 | 31 |   |   |   |

# Procrastinator Tip

Procrastination might be counter-productive, but working all the time is counterintuitive.

Things I have to do but that can wait a day, or two, or three . . .

Small things I have to do before I can do the big things I have to do

Things I absolutely have to do unless I absolutely don't want to do them

Things people have been bugging me to do for a really long time

doodle block

# july

monday
## 15 196

tuesday
◑ **16** 197

wednesday
## 17 198

thursday
## 18 199

friday
## 19 200

saturday
## 20 201

sunday
## 21 202

# Procrastinator Wisdom

 I've got my priorities straight—it's my timeline that keeps taking detours.

**Things I have to do but that can wait a day, or two, or three . . .**

**Small things I have to do before I can do the big things I have to do**

**Things I absolutely have to do unless I absolutely don't want to do them**

**Things people have been bugging me to do for a really long time**

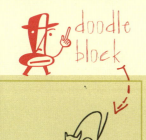

doodle
block

# july

*monday*
○ **22** 203

*tuesday*
**23** 204

*wednesday*
**24** 205

*thursday*
**25** 206

*friday*
**26** 207

*saturday*
**27** 208

*sunday*
**28** 209

july

| s | m | t | w | t | f | s |
|---|---|---|---|---|---|---|
|   |   | 1 | 2 | 3 | 4 | 5 | 6 |
| 7 | 8 | 9 | 10 | 11 | 12 | 13 |
| 14 | 15 | 16 | 17 | 18 | 19 | 20 |
| 21 | 22 | 23 | 24 | 25 | 26 | 27 |
| 28 | 29 | 30 | 31 |   |   |   |

# Procrastinator Tip

If you come to a fork in the road, find the nearest market, buy some delicious food, and have yourself a picnic.

**Things I have to do but that can wait a day, or two, or three . . .**

**Small things I have to do before I can do the big things I have to do**

**Things I absolutely have to do unless I absolutely don't want to do them**

**Things people have been bugging me to do for a really long time**

 doodle
block

# jul / aug

| | *monday* |
|---|---|
| ◗ | **29** 210 |

*tuesday*
**30** 211

*wednesday*
**31** 212

*thursday*
**1** 213

*friday*
**2** 214

*saturday*
**3** 215

*sunday*
**4** 216

# Procrastinator Tip

A to-do list is not an official to-do list until it becomes an overdue list.

**Things I have to do but that can wait a day, or two, or three . . .**

**Small things I have to do before I can do the big things I have to do**

**Things I absolutely have to do unless I absolutely don't want to do them**

**Things people have been bugging me to do for a really long time**

doodle
block

# august

CIVIC HOLIDAY (CANADA, MOST PROVINCES)
BANK HOLIDAY (SCOTLAND)

*monday*
**5** 217

*tuesday*
● **6** 218

*wednesday*
**7** 219

*thursday*
**8** 220

*friday*
**9** 221

*saturday*
**10** 222

*sunday*
**11** 223

## august

| s | m | t | w | t | f | s |
|---|---|---|---|---|---|---|
|   |   |   |   | 1 | 2 | 3 |
| 4 | 5 | 6 | 7 | 8 | 9 | 10 |
| 11 | 12 | 13 | 14 | 15 | 16 | 17 |
| 18 | 19 | 20 | 21 | 22 | 23 | 24 |
| 25 | 26 | 27 | 28 | 29 | 30 | 31 |

# The Perfect Procrastinator's Soundtrack

1. "Grooving" by the Young Rascals
2. "Up on the Roof" by the Drifters
3. "Sitting on the Dock of the Bay" by Otis Redding
4. "Day Tripper" by the Beatles
5. "Summer Wind" by Frank Sinatra
6. "Summer in the City" by the Lovin' Spoonful
7. "Margaritaville" by Jimmy Buffett
8. "Mexico" by James Taylor
9. "Saturday in the Park" by Chicago
10. "Summer Breeze" by Seals and Crofts

# Invent five words that mean "wonderful" and five words that mean "ridiculous."

1. _____

2. _____

3. _____

4. _____

5. _____

6. _____

7. _____

8. _____

9. _____

10. _____

# Procrastinator Wisdom

The word "procrastination" first appeared in 1909 in the *Oxford English Dictionary*, nearly a century before words like "time frame" and "multitasking" made their debuts.

Things I have to do but that can wait a day, or two, or three . . .

Small things I have to do before I can do the big things I have to do

Things I absolutely have to do unless I absolutely don't want to do them

Things people have been bugging me to do for a really long time

doodle block

# august

*tuesday*
**13** 225

*wednesday*
◑ **14** 226

*thursday*
**15** 227

*friday*
**16** 228

*saturday*
**17** 229

*sunday*
**18** 230

**august**

| s | m | t | w | t | f | s |
|---|---|---|---|---|---|---|
|   |   |   |   | 1 | 2 | 3 |
| 4 | 5 | 6 | 7 | 8 | 9 | 10 |
| 11 | 12 | 13 | 14 | 15 | 16 | 17 |
| 18 | 19 | 20 | 21 | 22 | 23 | 24 |
| 25 | 26 | 27 | 28 | 29 | 30 | 31 |

# Procrastinator Tip

Procrastination is a state of mind.
If you don't mind, it doesn't matter.

**Things I have to do but that can wait a day, or two, or three . . .**

**Small things I have to do before I can do the big things I have to do**

**Things I absolutely have to do unless I absolutely don't want to do them**

**Things people have been bugging me to do for a really long time**

doodle block

# august

*monday*
## 19 231

*tuesday*
## 20 232

*wednesday*
## ○ 21 233

*thursday*
## 22 234

*friday*
## 23 235

*saturday*
## 24 236

*sunday*
## 25 237

### august

| s | m | t | w | t | f | s |
|---|---|---|---|---|---|---|
|   |   |   |   | 1 | 2 | 3 |
| 4 | 5 | 6 | 7 | 8 | 9 | 10 |
| 11 | 12 | 13 | 14 | 15 | 16 | 17 |
| 18 | 19 | 20 | 21 | 22 | 23 | 24 |
| 25 | 26 | 27 | 28 | 29 | 30 | 31 |

# Procrastinator Tip

Side effects of procrastinating include good times, less work, and fewer people expecting things of you.

**Things I have to do but that can wait a day, or two, or three . . .**

**Small things I have to do before I can do the big things I have to do**

**Things I absolutely have to do unless I absolutely don't want to do them**

**Things people have been bugging me to do for a really long time**

doodle block

# aug / sep

BANK HOLIDAY (UK EXCEPT SCOTLAND)

*monday*
**26** 238

*tuesday*
**27** 239

*wednesday*
◑ **28** 240

*thursday*
**29** 241

*friday*
**30** 242

*saturday*
**31** 243

*sunday*
**1** 244

**september**

| s | m | t | w | t | f | s |
|---|---|---|---|---|---|---|
| 1 | 2 | 3 | 4 | 5 | 6 | 7 |
| 8 | 9 | 10 | 11 | 12 | 13 | 14 |
| 15 | 16 | 17 | 18 | 19 | 20 | 21 |
| 22 | 23 | 24 | 25 | 26 | 27 | 28 |
| 29 | 30 | | | | | |

# Procrastinator Wisdom

*It's not when you get something done, it's what you do on the way to getting something done that you'll remember.*

**Things I have to do but that can wait a day, or two, or three . . .**

**Small things I have to do before I can do the big things I have to do**

**Things I absolutely have to do unless I absolutely don't want to do them**

**Things people have been bugging me to do for a really long time**

 doodle block

# september

LABOR DAY (US, CANADA)

*monday*
2  245

*tuesday*
3  246

ROSH HASHANAH (BEGINS AT SUNSET)

*wednesday*
4  247

*thursday*
● 5  248

*friday*
6  249

*saturday*
7  250

*sunday*
8  251

## september

| s | m | t | w | t | f | s |
|---|---|---|---|---|---|---|
|   | 1 | 2 | 3 | 4 | 5 | 6 | 7 |
| 8 | 9 | 10 | 11 | 12 | 13 | 14 |
| 15 | 16 | 17 | 18 | 19 | 20 | 21 |
| 22 | 23 | 24 | 25 | 26 | 27 | 28 |
| 29 | 30 |  |  |  |  |  |

# Debunking Myths About Procrastination

1. Procrastination feels good initially, but in the end you're only screwing yourself. *Well, what's wrong with a little self-pleasure every once in a while?*

2. Procrastination destroys teamwork in the workplace. *That all depends on how many procrastinators there are on your team.*

3. Procrastination is a form of rebellion. *Don't most noteworthy achievers buck the system?*

4. Procrastination predicts higher consumption of alcohol among those who drink. *You've got to do something when you're surrounded by uptight, deadline-driven people.*

5. Procrastinators lie to themselves. *At least they don't lie to others.*

6. Procrastinators search for distractions that don't take a lot of commitment on their part. *We're procrastinators, not saints.*

7. The longer you wait to tackle a task, the harder it becomes to complete. *True, but the easier it becomes to ignore.*

8. Procrastination is a curable addiction. *So is eating sugar, but I'm enjoying a delicious hot fudge sundae as I type this.*

9. Procrastinators are often perfectionists. *What's wrong with being entirely without flaws, defects, or shortcomings?*

10. Procrastinators often find the most difficult way to do something. *And for this we're called lazy?!*

# List 10 thoughts nobody would ever think would be in your head.

1. _____

2. _____

3. _____

4. _____

5. _____

6. _____

7. _____

8. _____

9. _____

10. _____

# Procrastinator Wisdom

A long time ago I tried the "now" habit. It didn't give me much to look forward to.

Things I have to do but that can wait a day, or two, or three . . .

Small things I have to do before I can do the big things I have to do

Things I absolutely have to do unless I absolutely don't want to do them

Things people have been bugging me to do for a really long time

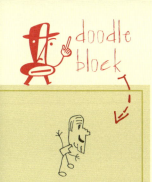

doodle block

# september

monday
**9**  252

tuesday
**10**  253

wednesday
**11**  254

thursday
◑ **12**  255

YOM KIPPUR (BEGINS AT SUNSET)

friday
**13**  256

saturday
**14**  257

sunday
**15**  258

**september**

| s | m | t | w | t | f | s |
|---|---|---|---|---|---|---|
| | 1 | 2 | 3 | 4 | 5 | 6 | 7 |
| 8 | 9 | 10 | 11 | 12 | 13 | 14 |
| 15 | 16 | 17 | 18 | 19 | 20 | 21 |
| 22 | 23 | 24 | 25 | 26 | 27 | 28 |
| 29 | 30 | | | | | |

# Procrastinator Tip

What is never begun can live forever in spirit.

Things I have to do but that can wait a day, or two, or three . . .

Small things I have to do before I can do the big things I have to do

Things I absolutely have to do unless I absolutely don't want to do them

Things people have been bugging me to do for a really long time

doodle
block

# september

INTERNATIONAL DAY OF PEACE

AUTUMNAL EQUINOX 20:44 UTC

## september

| s | m | t | w | t | f | s |
|---|---|---|---|---|---|---|
| 1 | 2 | 3 | 4 | 5 | 6 | 7 |
| 8 | 9 | 10 | 11 | 12 | 13 | 14 |
| 15 | 16 | 17 | 18 | 19 | 20 | 21 |
| 22 | 23 | 24 | 25 | 26 | 27 | 28 |
| 29 | 30 | | | | | |

# Procrastinator Tip

If you never procrastinate, aren't you in danger of overworking?

Things I have to do but that can wait a day, or two, or three . . .

Small things I have to do before I can do the big things I have to do

Things I absolutely have to do unless I absolutely don't want to do them

Things people have been bugging me to do for a really long time

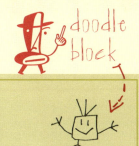

doodle block

# september

## september

| s | m | t | w | t | f | s |
|---|---|---|---|---|---|---|
| 1 | 2 | 3 | 4 | 5 | 6 | 7 |
| 8 | 9 | 10 | 11 | 12 | 13 | 14 |
| 15 | 16 | 17 | 18 | 19 | 20 | 21 |
| 22 | 23 | 24 | 25 | 26 | 27 | 28 |
| 29 | 30 | | | | | |

# Procrastinator Tip

There's only one solution when you are totally stressed out with a million things to do: take a nap!

**Things I have to do but that can wait a day, or two, or three . . .**

**Small things I have to do before I can do the big things I have to do**

**Things I absolutely have to do unless I absolutely don't want to do them**

**Things people have been bugging me to do for a really long time**

doodle
block

# sep / oct

| | |
|---|---|
| *monday* | |
| **30** | 273 |
| *tuesday* | |
| **1** | 274 |
| *wednesday* | |
| **2** | 275 |
| *thursday* | |
| **3** | 276 |
| *friday* | |
| **4** | 277 |
| *saturday* | |
| ● **5** | 278 |
| *sunday* | |
| **6** | 279 |

**october**

| s | m | t | w | t | f | s |
|---|---|---|---|---|---|---|
| | | | 1 | 2 | 3 | 4 | 5 |
| 6 | 7 | 8 | 9 | 10 | 11 | 12 |
| 13 | 14 | 15 | 16 | 17 | 18 | 19 |
| 20 | 21 | 22 | 23 | 24 | 25 | 26 |
| 27 | 28 | 29 | 30 | 31 | | |

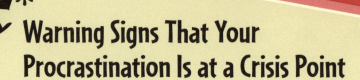

## Warning Signs That Your Procrastination Is at a Crisis Point

1. You've made a master list for all of your lists.

2. You consider jumping from one idea to the next to be exercise.

3. You can't get through a half hour of work without doodling or daydreaming.

4. You reorganized your desk shortly after you reorganized your desk.

5. You've made color-coded 3 x 5 index cards for each item on your to-do list.

6. You've asked your dog or cat for their opinion on your work.

7. You've convinced yourself that playing Minesweeper on your laptop is making you smarter.

8. You're thinking about where you'll go for lunch before you've finished breakfast.

9. You send an e-mail to yourself just to make sure your e-mail is working.

10. Every time you receive an e-mail, you check for new e-mail twice.

# Name the 10 things you miss most about being a kid.

1. _____

2. _____

3. _____

4. _____

5. _____

6. _____

7. _____

8. _____

9. _____

10. _____

# Procrastinator Tip

Checking your e-mail and visiting your home page every 10 minutes make you a very informed person.

**Things I have to do but that can wait a day, or two, or three . . .**

**Small things I have to do before I can do the big things I have to do**

**Things I absolutely have to do unless I absolutely don't want to do them**

**Things people have been bugging me to do for a really long time**

doodle
block

# october

*monday*
**7** <sub></sub> 280

*tuesday*
**8** 281

*wednesday*
**9** 282

*thursday*
**10** 283

*friday*
◐ **11** 284

*saturday*
**12** 285

*sunday*
**13** 286

## october

| s | m | t | w | t | f | s |
|---|---|---|---|---|---|---|
|   |   |   | 1 | 2 | 3 | 4 | 5 |
| 6 | 7 | 8 | 9 | 10 | 11 | 12 |
| 13 | 14 | 15 | 16 | 17 | 18 | 19 |
| 20 | 21 | 22 | 23 | 24 | 25 | 26 |
| 27 | 28 | 29 | 30 | 31 |   |   |

# Procrastinator Wisdom

Time is like a raging river—you can't manage it; you can only let it run free.

**Things I have to do but that can wait a day, or two, or three . . .**

**Small things I have to do before I can do the big things I have to do**

**Things I absolutely have to do unless I absolutely don't want to do them**

**Things people have been bugging me to do for a really long time**

doodle block

# october

COLUMBUS DAY

THANKSGIVING DAY (CANADA)

*monday*
**14**  287

*tuesday*
**15**  288

*wednesday*
**16**  289

*thursday*
**17**  290

*friday*
○ **18**  291

*saturday*
**19**  292

*sunday*
**20**  293

## october

| s | m | t | w | t | f | s |
|---|---|---|---|---|---|---|
|   |   | 1 | 2 | 3 | 4 | 5 |
| 6 | 7 | 8 | 9 | 10 | 11 | 12 |
| 13 | 14 | 15 | 16 | 17 | 18 | 19 |
| 20 | 21 | 22 | 23 | 24 | 25 | 26 |
| 27 | 28 | 29 | 30 | 31 |   |   |

# Procrastinator Wisdom

I'd rather be overly lazy than overworked any day.

**Things I have to do but that can wait a day, or two, or three . . .**

**Small things I have to do before I can do the big things I have to do**

**Things I absolutely have to do unless I absolutely don't want to do them**

**Things people have been bugging me to do for a really long time**

doodle block

# october

monday
## 21 294

tuesday
## 22 295

wednesday
## 23 296

UNITED NATIONS DAY

thursday
## 24 297

friday
## 25 298

saturday
◗ ## 26 299

SUMMER TIME ENDS (UK)

sunday
## 27 300

# Procrastinator Tip

Life is fragile. Work with caution.

Things I have to do but that can wait a day, or two, or three . . .

Small things I have to do before I can do the big things I have to do

Things I absolutely have to do unless I absolutely don't want to do them

Things people have been bugging me to do for a really long time

doodle block

*monday*
**28**  301

*tuesday*
**29**  302

*wednesday*
**30**  303

HALLOWEEN                                              *thursday*
**31**  304

*friday*
**1**  305

*saturday*
**2**  306

| s | m | t | w | t | f | s |
|---|---|---|---|---|---|---|
|   |   |   |   |   | 1 | 2 |
| 3 | 4 | 5 | 6 | 7 | 8 | 9 |
| 10 | 11 | 12 | 13 | 14 | 15 | 16 |
| 17 | 18 | 19 | 20 | 21 | 22 | 23 |
| 24 | 25 | 26 | 27 | 28 | 29 | 30 |

DAYLIGHT SAVING TIME ENDS                              *sunday*
● **3**  307

# Procrastinator Wisdom

Monday was going to be my last day of procrastination. Somehow it lasted all week.

**Things I have to do but that can wait a day, or two, or three . . .**

**Small things I have to do before I can do the big things I have to do**

**Things I absolutely have to do unless I absolutely don't want to do them**

**Things people have been bugging me to do for a really long time**

doodle block

# november

monday
## 4 308

tuesday
## 5 309

wednesday
## 6 310

thursday
## 7 311

friday
## 8 312

saturday
## 9 313

sunday
## ◑ 10 314

### november

| s | m | t | w | t | f | s |
|---|---|---|---|---|---|---|
|   |   |   |   |   | 1 | 2 |
| 3 | 4 | 5 | 6 | 7 | 8 | 9 |
| 10 | 11 | 12 | 13 | 14 | 15 | 16 |
| 17 | 18 | 19 | 20 | 21 | 22 | 23 |
| 24 | 25 | 26 | 27 | 28 | 29 | 30 |

# Killer Excuses for Arriving Late to Work

1. I left the office so late last night that I got locked in the garage. When they opened the garage this morning, I rushed home to shower and came back ASAP.

2. In the middle of the night my dog threw up on my nightstand, and I didn't realize it killed my alarm clock.

3. I started working from home early this morning and didn't want to break my flow.

4. Believe it or not, I was early. I was working on my laptop, sitting on the floor behind my desk. Sometimes I think better there.

5. My spouse surprised me with breakfast in bed. No, that's not all, but frankly, it's none of your business.

6. I was a key witness to a crime on my way here. Never mind, it's too upsetting to talk about. Yes, I'm all right. No, it won't be on the news tonight.

7. I helped an old lady cross the street, and she insisted on buying me coffee and telling me about her medical conditions.

8. I decided that instead of taking sick days, I'd come in late every now and then.

9. I rode my bike. Yes, on the freeway.

10. You told me not to come back until I finished my work.

# List five jobs you wish you could do and five jobs you hope you never have to do.

1. _____

2. _____

3. _____

4. _____

5. _____

6. _____

7. _____

8. _____

9. _____

10. _____

# Procrastinator Tip

Doing nothing is actually doing something. Trust your gut: if it feels like you should stop working, do so immediately.

Things I have to do but that can wait a day, or two, or three . . .

Small things I have to do before I can do the big things I have to do

Things I absolutely have to do unless I absolutely don't want to do them

Things people have been bugging me to do for a really long time

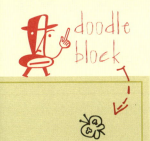

doodle block

# november

VETERANS DAY
REMEMBRANCE DAY (CANADA)

*monday*
**11** 315

*tuesday*
**12** 316

*wednesday*
**13** 317

*thursday*
**14** 318

*friday*
**15** 319

*saturday*
**16** 320

*sunday*
○ **17** 321

### november

| s | m | t | w | t | f | s |
|---|---|---|---|---|---|---|
| | | | | | 1 | 2 |
| 3 | 4 | 5 | 6 | 7 | 8 | 9 |
| 10 | 11 | 12 | 13 | 14 | 15 | 16 |
| 17 | 18 | 19 | 20 | 21 | 22 | 23 |
| 24 | 25 | 26 | 27 | 28 | 29 | 30 |

# Procrastinator Wisdom

Some say procrastinators are hoarders who can't part with their mess. I say they're archivists.

**Things I have to do but that can wait a day, or two, or three . . .**

**Small things I have to do before I can do the big things I have to do**

**Things I absolutely have to do unless I absolutely don't want to do them**

**Things people have been bugging me to do for a really long time**

 doodle block

# november

*tuesday*
## 19 323

*wednesday*
## 20 324

*thursday*
## 21 325

*friday*
## 22 326

*saturday*
## 23 327

### november

| s | m | t | w | t | f | s |
|---|---|---|---|---|---|---|
|   |   |   |   |   | 1 | 2 |
| 3 | 4 | 5 | 6 | 7 | 8 | 9 |
| 10 | 11 | 12 | 13 | 14 | 15 | 16 |
| 17 | 18 | 19 | 20 | 21 | 22 | 23 |
| 24 | 25 | 26 | 27 | 28 | 29 | 30 |

*sunday*
## 24 328

# Procrastinator Wisdom

 The brain is a muscle that works best in short spurts.

**Things I have to do but that can wait a day, or two, or three . . .**

**Small things I have to do before I can do the big things I have to do**

**Things I absolutely have to do unless I absolutely don't want to do them**

**Things people have been bugging me to do for a really long time**

doodle
block

*monday*
◐ **25** 329

*tuesday*
**26** 330

HANUKKAH (BEGINS AT SUNSET)
*wednesday*
**27** 331

THANKSGIVING
*thursday*
**28** 332

*friday*
**29** 333

ST. ANDREW'S DAY (SCOTLAND)
*saturday*
**30** 334

*sunday*
**1** 335

## december

| s | m | t | w | t | f | s |
|---|---|---|---|---|---|---|
| | 1 | 2 | 3 | 4 | 5 | 6 | 7 |
| 8 | 9 | 10 | 11 | 12 | 13 | 14 |
| 15 | 16 | 17 | 18 | 19 | 20 | 21 |
| 22 | 23 | 24 | 25 | 26 | 27 | 28 |
| 29 | 30 | 31 | | | | |

# Procrastinator Wisdom

You can spend time, you can share time, and you can waste time, but can you really manage time? It sounds a little arrogant to me.

**Things I have to do but that can wait a day, or two, or three . . .**

**Small things I have to do before I can do the big things I have to do**

**Things I absolutely have to do unless I absolutely don't want to do them**

**Things people have been bugging me to do for a really long time**

doodle block

# december

ST. ANDREW'S DAY BANK HOLIDAY (SCOTLAND)

*monday*
2 · 336

*tuesday*
● 3 · 337

*wednesday*
4 · 338

*thursday*
5 · 339

*friday*
6 · 340

*saturday*
7 · 341

*sunday*
8 · 342

## december

| s | m | t | w | t | f | s |
|---|---|---|---|---|---|---|
| 1 | 2 | 3 | 4 | 5 | 6 | 7 |
| 8 | 9 | 10 | 11 | 12 | 13 | 14 |
| 15 | 16 | 17 | 18 | 19 | 20 | 21 |
| 22 | 23 | 24 | 25 | 26 | 27 | 28 |
| 29 | 30 | 31 | | | | |

# How to Handle Mondays

1. Remember, Monday's only purpose is to lead to Tuesday.

2. Tell yourself you have another four workdays to make up for a miserably unproductive day.

3. Plot and plan, but never implement.

4. Keep in mind that if you don't do a single thing, you'll be in good company.

5. Use Monday as an excuse to organize your desk and files.

6. Take a long lunch and make believe it's Friday.

7. Use it as it was intended: a day to reacclimate yourself to the workplace.

8. Take advantage of one of the Internet's busiest shopping days.

9. Read blogs and tweets by fellow Monday-haters.

10. Memorize the lyrics to the Mamas and the Papas song "Monday, Monday."

# List 10 things you'd include in your dream kitchen.

1. _____

2. _____

3. _____

4. _____

5. _____

6. _____

7. _____

8. _____

9. _____

10. _____

# Procrastinator Tip

If you don't feel like doing it, it won't feel like you did it when you do it.

**Things I have to do but that can wait a day, or two, or three . . .**

**Small things I have to do before I can do the big things I have to do**

**Things I absolutely have to do unless I absolutely don't want to do them**

**Things people have been bugging me to do for a really long time**

doodle block

# december

*monday*
◖ 9   343

*tuesday*
10   344

*wednesday*
11   345

*thursday*
12   346

*friday*
13   347

*saturday*
14   348

*sunday*
15   349

## december

| s | m | t | w | t | f | s |
|---|---|---|---|---|---|---|
| 1 | 2 | 3 | 4 | 5 | 6 | 7 |
| 8 | 9 | 10 | 11 | 12 | 13 | 14 |
| 15 | 16 | 17 | 18 | 19 | 20 | 21 |
| 22 | 23 | 24 | 25 | 26 | 27 | 28 |
| 29 | 30 | 31 | | | | |

# Procrastinator Wisdom

If there are so many cons to procrastination, why does the word start with "pro"?

**Things I have to do but that can wait a day, or two, or three . . .**

**Small things I have to do before I can do the big things I have to do**

**Things I absolutely have to do unless I absolutely don't want to do them**

**Things people have been bugging me to do for a really long time**

doodle block

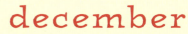

# december

*tuesday*
○ **17** 351

*wednesday*
**18** 352

*thursday*
**19** 353

*friday*
**20** 354

WINTER SOLSTICE 17:11 UTC

*saturday*
**21** 355

*sunday*
**22** 356

## december

| s | m | t | w | t | f | s |
|---|---|---|---|---|---|---|
| | 1 | 2 | 3 | 4 | 5 | 6 | 7 |
| 8 | 9 | 10 | 11 | 12 | 13 | 14 |
| 15 | 16 | 17 | 18 | 19 | 20 | 21 |
| 22 | 23 | 24 | 25 | 26 | 27 | 28 |
| 29 | 30 | 31 | | | | |

# Procrastinator Wisdom

No ifs, ands, or buts about it: one day I might stop procrastinating.

**Things I have to do but that can wait a day, or two, or three . . .**

**Small things I have to do before I can do the big things I have to do**

**Things I absolutely have to do unless I absolutely don't want to do them**

**Things people have been bugging me to do for a really long time**

doodle
block

# december

CHRISTMAS
BANK HOLIDAY (CANADA, UK)

KWANZAA BEGINS
BOXING DAY (CANADA, UK)

### december

| s | m | t | w | t | f | s |
|---|---|---|---|---|---|---|
|   | 1 | 2 | 3 | 4 | 5 | 6 | 7 |
| 8 | 9 | 10 | 11 | 12 | 13 | 14 |
| 15 | 16 | 17 | 18 | 19 | 20 | 21 |
| 22 | 23 | 24 | 25 | 26 | 27 | 28 |
| 29 | 30 | 31 |   |   |   |   |

# Procrastinator Tip

The art of doing nothing is an art. Respect and cultivate it whenever you can.

**Things I have to do but that can wait a day, or two, or three . . .**

**Small things I have to do before I can do the big things I have to do**

**Things I absolutely have to do unless I absolutely don't want to do them**

**Things people have been bugging me to do for a really long time**

doodle block

# dec / jan 2014

*monday*
**30** 364

*tuesday*
**31** 365

NEW YEAR'S DAY
BANK HOLIDAY (CANADA, UK)

*wednesday*
● **1** 1

BANK HOLIDAY (SCOTLAND)

*thursday*
**2** 2

*friday*
**3** 3

*saturday*
**4** 4

*sunday*
**5** 5

## january 2014

| s | m | t | w | t | f | s |
|---|---|---|---|---|---|---|
|   |   |   | 1 | 2 | 3 | 4 |
| 5 | 6 | 7 | 8 | 9 | 10 | 11 |
| 12 | 13 | 14 | 15 | 16 | 17 | 18 |
| 19 | 20 | 21 | 22 | 23 | 24 | 25 |
| 26 | 27 | 28 | 29 | 30 | 31 |   |

# Procrastinator Tip

The best way to appreciate the passage of time is to idly watch it pass.

**Things I have to do but that can wait a day, or two, or three . . .**

**Small things I have to do before I can do the big things I have to do**

**Things I absolutely have to do unless I absolutely don't want to do them**

**Things people have been bugging me to do for a really long time**

# january 2014

*monday*
## 6 6

*tuesday*
## 7 7

*wednesday*
◑ ## 8 8

*thursday*
## 9 9

*friday*
## 10 10

*saturday*
## 11 11

*sunday*
## 12 12

## january 2014

| s | m | t | w | t | f | s |
|---|---|---|---|---|---|---|
|   |   |   | 1 | 2 | 3 | 4 |
| 5 | 6 | 7 | 8 | 9 | 10 | 11 |
| 12 | 13 | 14 | 15 | 16 | 17 | 18 |
| 19 | 20 | 21 | 22 | 23 | 24 | 25 |
| 26 | 27 | 28 | 29 | 30 | 31 |   |

## Grace Periods for Bills Due, and/or Tax Extension Schedule/Plan

1. _____

2. _____

3. _____

4. _____

5. _____

6. _____

7. _____

8. _____

9. _____

10. _____

# People to Call
# When I Don't Feel Like Working

| NAME | PHONE (H) |
| | PHONE (W) |
| | PAGER |
| | CELL |

| NAME | PHONE (H) |
| | PHONE (W) |
| | PAGER |
| | CELL |

| NAME | PHONE (H) |
| | PHONE (W) |
| | PAGER |
| | CELL |

| NAME | PHONE (H) |
| | PHONE (W) |
| | PAGER |
| | CELL |

# 2014

## JANUARY

| s | m | t | w | t | f | s |
|---|---|---|---|---|---|---|
| | | | 1 | 2 | 3 | 4 |
| 5 | 6 | 7 | 8 | 9 | 10 | 11 |
| 12 | 13 | 14 | 15 | 16 | 17 | 18 |
| 19 | 20 | 21 | 22 | 23 | 24 | 25 |
| 26 | 27 | 28 | 29 | 30 | 31 | |

## FEBRUARY

| s | m | t | w | t | f | s |
|---|---|---|---|---|---|---|
| | | | | | | 1 |
| 2 | 3 | 4 | 5 | 6 | 7 | 8 |
| 9 | 10 | 11 | 12 | 13 | 14 | 15 |
| 16 | 17 | 18 | 19 | 20 | 21 | 22 |
| 23 | 24 | 25 | 26 | 27 | 28 | |

## MARCH

| s | m | t | w | t | f | s |
|---|---|---|---|---|---|---|
| | | | | | | 1 |
| 2 | 3 | 4 | 5 | 6 | 7 | 8 |
| 9 | 10 | 11 | 12 | 13 | 14 | 15 |
| 16 | 17 | 18 | 19 | 20 | 21 | 22 |
| 23 | 24 | 25 | 26 | 27 | 28 | 29 |
| 30 | 31 | | | | | |

## APRIL

| s | m | t | w | t | f | s |
|---|---|---|---|---|---|---|
| | | 1 | 2 | 3 | 4 | 5 |
| 6 | 7 | 8 | 9 | 10 | 11 | 12 |
| 13 | 14 | 15 | 16 | 17 | 18 | 19 |
| 20 | 21 | 22 | 23 | 24 | 25 | 26 |
| 27 | 28 | 29 | 30 | | | |

## MAY

| s | m | t | w | t | f | s |
|---|---|---|---|---|---|---|
| | | | | 1 | 2 | 3 |
| 4 | 5 | 6 | 7 | 8 | 9 | 10 |
| 11 | 12 | 13 | 14 | 15 | 16 | 17 |
| 18 | 19 | 20 | 21 | 22 | 23 | 24 |
| 25 | 26 | 27 | 28 | 29 | 30 | 31 |

## JUNE

| s | m | t | w | t | f | s |
|---|---|---|---|---|---|---|
| 1 | 2 | 3 | 4 | 5 | 6 | 7 |
| 8 | 9 | 10 | 11 | 12 | 13 | 14 |
| 15 | 16 | 17 | 18 | 19 | 20 | 21 |
| 22 | 23 | 24 | 25 | 26 | 27 | 28 |
| 29 | 30 | | | | | |

## JULY

| s | m | t | w | t | f | s |
|---|---|---|---|---|---|---|
| | | 1 | 2 | 3 | 4 | 5 |
| 6 | 7 | 8 | 9 | 10 | 11 | 12 |
| 13 | 14 | 15 | 16 | 17 | 18 | 19 |
| 20 | 21 | 22 | 23 | 24 | 25 | 26 |
| 27 | 28 | 29 | 30 | 31 | | |

## AUGUST

| s | m | t | w | t | f | s |
|---|---|---|---|---|---|---|
| | | | | | 1 | 2 |
| 3 | 4 | 5 | 6 | 7 | 8 | 9 |
| 10 | 11 | 12 | 13 | 14 | 15 | 16 |
| 17 | 18 | 19 | 20 | 21 | 22 | 23 |
| 24 | 25 | 26 | 27 | 28 | 29 | 30 |
| 31 | | | | | | |

## SEPTEMBER

| s | m | t | w | t | f | s |
|---|---|---|---|---|---|---|
| | 1 | 2 | 3 | 4 | 5 | 6 |
| 7 | 8 | 9 | 10 | 11 | 12 | 13 |
| 14 | 15 | 16 | 17 | 18 | 19 | 20 |
| 21 | 22 | 23 | 24 | 25 | 26 | 27 |
| 28 | 29 | 30 | | | | |

## OCTOBER

| s | m | t | w | t | f | s |
|---|---|---|---|---|---|---|
| | | | 1 | 2 | 3 | 4 |
| 5 | 6 | 7 | 8 | 9 | 10 | 11 |
| 12 | 13 | 14 | 15 | 16 | 17 | 18 |
| 19 | 20 | 21 | 22 | 23 | 24 | 25 |
| 26 | 27 | 28 | 29 | 30 | 31 | |

## NOVEMBER

| s | m | t | w | t | f | s |
|---|---|---|---|---|---|---|
| | | | | | | 1 |
| 2 | 3 | 4 | 5 | 6 | 7 | 8 |
| 9 | 10 | 11 | 12 | 13 | 14 | 15 |
| 16 | 17 | 18 | 19 | 20 | 21 | 22 |
| 23 | 24 | 25 | 26 | 27 | 28 | 29 |
| 30 | | | | | | |

## DECEMBER

| s | m | t | w | t | f | s |
|---|---|---|---|---|---|---|
| | 1 | 2 | 3 | 4 | 5 | 6 |
| 7 | 8 | 9 | 10 | 11 | 12 | 13 |
| 14 | 15 | 16 | 17 | 18 | 19 | 20 |
| 21 | 22 | 23 | 24 | 25 | 26 | 27 |
| 28 | 29 | 30 | 31 | | | |